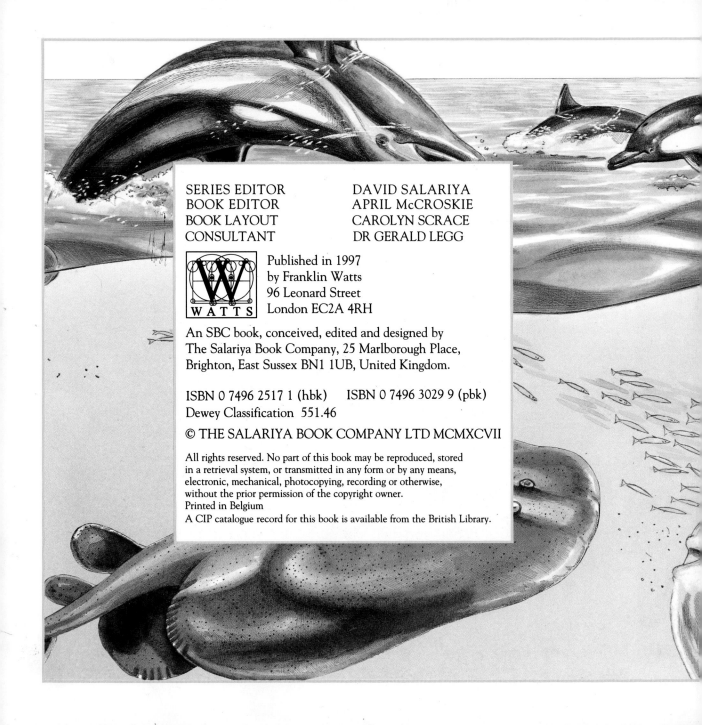

SERIES EDITOR   DAVID SALARIYA
BOOK EDITOR   APRIL McCROSKIE
BOOK LAYOUT   CAROLYN SCRACE
CONSULTANT   DR GERALD LEGG

Published in 1997
by Franklin Watts
96 Leonard Street
London EC2A 4RH

An SBC book, conceived, edited and designed by
The Salariya Book Company, 25 Marlborough Place,
Brighton, East Sussex BN1 1UB, United Kingdom.

ISBN 0 7496 2517 1 (hbk)   ISBN 0 7496 3029 9 (pbk)
Dewey Classification 551.46

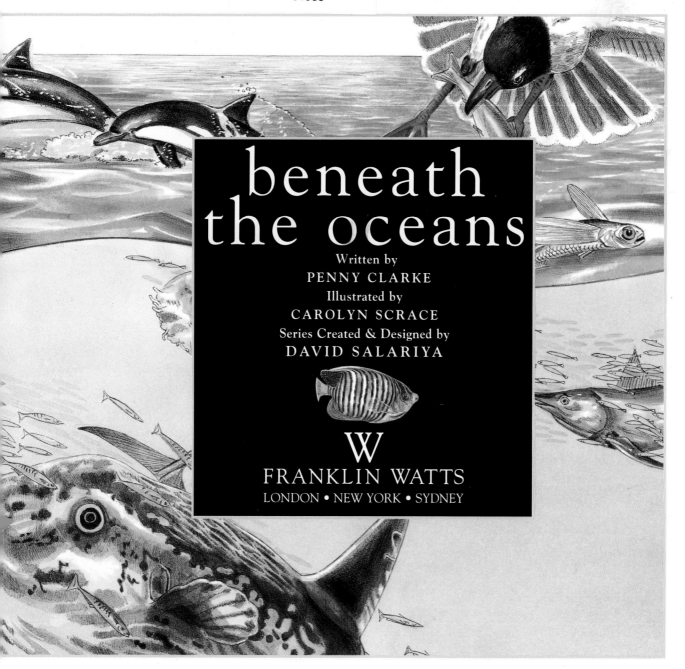

beneath
the oceans

Written by
PENNY CLARKE

Illustrated by
CAROLYN SCRACE

Series Created & Designed by
DAVID SALARIYA

W
FRANKLIN WATTS
LONDON • NEW YORK • SYDNEY

CONTENTS

Oceans are large basins in the Earth's surface which contain salt water. Today they cover over 70 per cent of the Earth. Seas are similar but smaller. If these basins were dry there would be no life on Earth, because scientists believe that life developed in the oceans and moved onto land much later.

Where did the water in the oceans originally come from? No one can be sure, but today much of it comes from deep within the Earth. When the volcanoes on the oceanbed erupt they pour out water from far beneath the oceans.

About 220 million years ago the Earth had just one vast ocean and one huge landmass. Then, about 100 million years ago, the landmass began to crack and the ocean water surged in. This was the beginning of today's continents and oceans. The process continues. An ocean is forming between Africa and Arabia as the land slowly drifts apart.

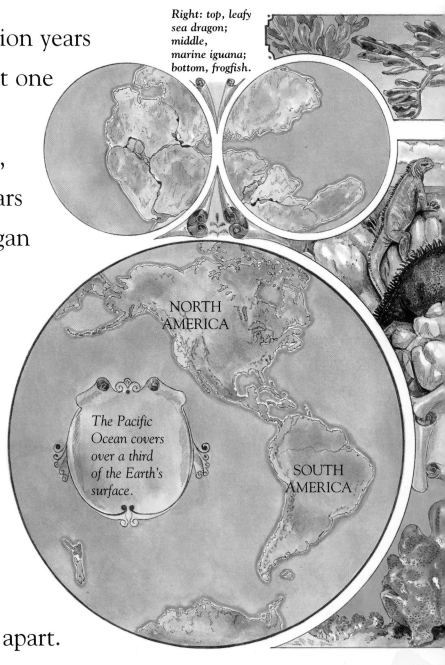

Right: top, leafy sea dragon; middle, marine iguana; bottom, frogfish.

NORTH AMERICA

The Pacific Ocean covers over a third of the Earth's surface.

SOUTH AMERICA

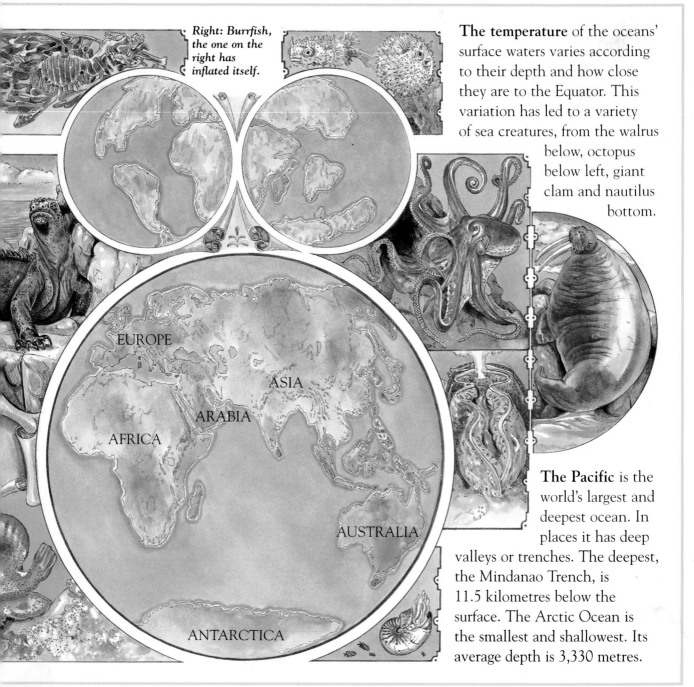

Right: Burrfish, the one on the right has inflated itself.

The temperature of the oceans' surface waters varies according to their depth and how close they are to the Equator. This variation has led to a variety of sea creatures, from the walrus below, octopus below left, giant clam and nautilus bottom.

EUROPE

ASIA

ARABIA

AFRICA

AUSTRALIA

ANTARCTICA

The Pacific is the world's largest and deepest ocean. In places it has deep valleys or trenches. The deepest, the Mindanao Trench, is 11.5 kilometres below the surface. The Arctic Ocean is the smallest and shallowest. Its average depth is 3,330 metres.

The pressure of the Earth's movements makes rocks buckle and bend. So the strata (layers) in which rock forms are seldom straight.

Scientists believe that the first huge continent split because of movements of the Earth's crust below the ocean. Much of the deep ocean floor is flat, but there are also mountain ranges. Pressure from deep within the Earth forces the oceanbed away from the ranges, and molten rock surfaces to form a

Mountain range on land

Strata

From time to time erupting volcanoes release the tremendous pressure that builds up deep within the Earth.

Molten rock coming to surface from Earth's core

Oceanbed going below landmass

When the oceanbed meets a landmass, the oceanbed eventually slides under the land.

new oceanbed. When the oceanbed meets a landmass the pressure makes the land push upwards. The Rockies and Andes mountains of North and South America were formed in this way.

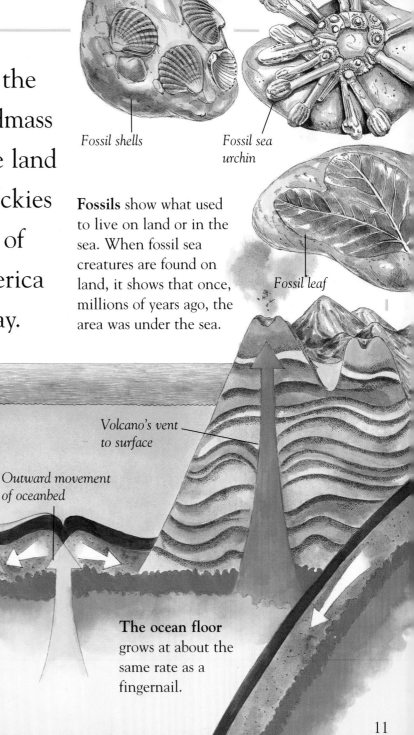

Fossil shells

Fossil sea urchin

Fossils show what used to live on land or in the sea. When fossil sea creatures are found on land, it shows that once, millions of years ago, the area was under the sea.

Fossil leaf

Volcano's vent to surface

Remains of undersea mountain

Outward movement of oceanbed

Earthquakes and active volcanoes are clues to activity at the Earth's centre, which is 6370 kilometres from the sea's surface.

The ocean floor grows at about the same rate as a fingernail.

WARM CURRENTS
COLD CURRENTS

Cold currents flow from the Arctic and Antarctic oceans towards the Equator. There they absorb warmth, before returning to the polar regions.

Chinstrap penguins

Penguins only live in the southern hemisphere.

Each ocean has a system of currents. These are strong movements of water caused by the Earth's rotation around the Sun.

North of the Equator most currents flow in a clockwise direction. South of the Equator they are anticlockwise.

Tides are mostly caused by the Moon, which pulls seawater towards it, away from the Earth. This causes a low tide.

On the opposite side of the world there is a corresponding high tide.

GREENLAND

NORTH
AMERICA

EUROPE

AFRICA

SOUTH
AMERICA

The cold polar oceans are particularly rich in sea creatures, from microscopic plankton to the huge whales that feed on it.

Sunlight makes the sea's surface light. But this light fades as you go deeper and many sea creatures live in pitch darkness.

Seas and

oceans are very dark. Sunlight can only reach to a depth of 180 metres – below that there is no light. But many creatures live in the ocean's darkness. Some make their own light. Others 'see' by feeling changes in pressure or currents. All can withstand low temperatures because water in the ocean depths is always cold, even if it is near the Equator.

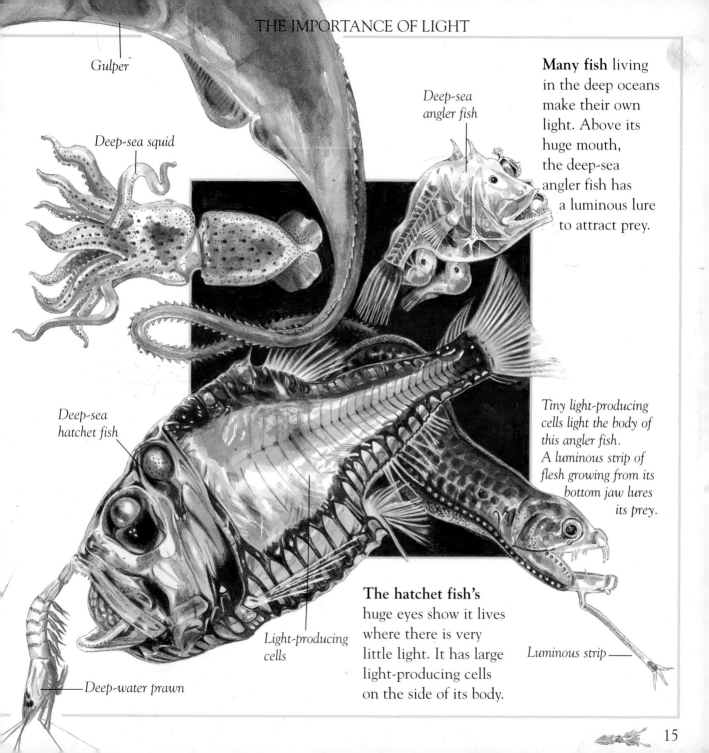

Gulper

Deep-sea squid

Deep-sea angler fish

Many fish living in the deep oceans make their own light. Above its huge mouth, the deep-sea angler fish has a luminous lure to attract prey.

Deep-sea hatchet fish

Tiny light-producing cells light the body of this angler fish. A luminous strip of flesh growing from its bottom jaw lures its prey.

The hatchet fish's huge eyes show it lives where there is very little light. It has large light-producing cells on the side of its body.

Light-producing cells

Luminous strip ——

Deep-water prawn

*Ganea
jellyfish*

Shoal of bonito

*Jellyfish
live in the
warmer
surface
waters of
the oceans.
Their young,
which are
called
medusae,
drift near
the surface.*

In mid-ocean sea temperatures change little. Differences in temperature between day and night only affect the first surface metre or so of water. Differences between summer and winter temperatures are felt to depths of 180 metres. Below that the temperature hardly changes. This makes a stable environment for sea creatures.

The electric ray has special cells in its body which can give electric shocks of up to 220 volts. It grows to 1.8 metres, but only has tiny teeth. Without its electric shock system it could not kill its prey.

Electric ray

Mako shark

Squid live mainly at depths of 180 to 1,650 metres. They are hunted by sperm whales.

Mako shark

The blue whale can be 32 metres long, but feeds entirely on plankton. The 4-metre long mako shark is a swift hunter, preying on mackerel, tuna and sardines.

Blue whale

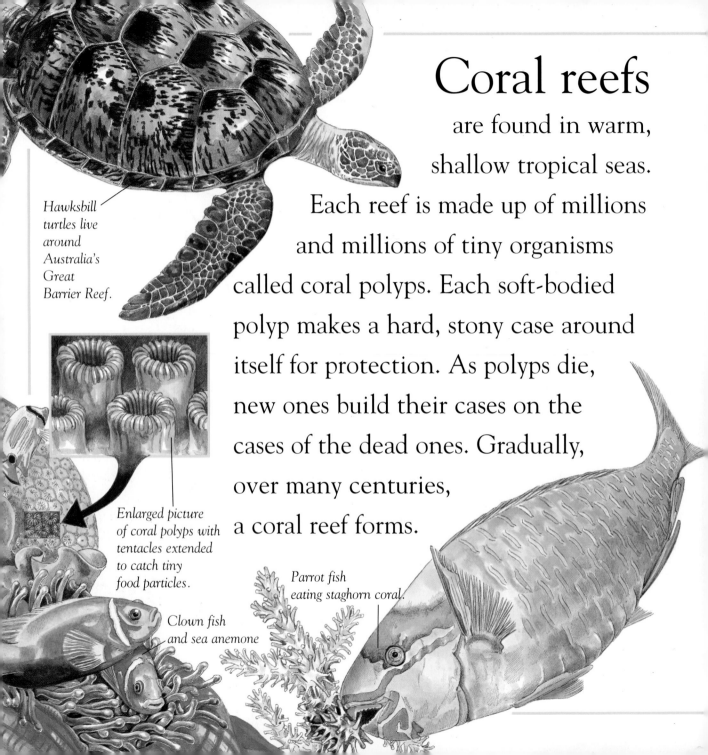

Coral reefs

are found in warm, shallow tropical seas. Each reef is made up of millions and millions of tiny organisms called coral polyps. Each soft-bodied polyp makes a hard, stony case around itself for protection. As polyps die, new ones build their cases on the cases of the dead ones. Gradually, over many centuries, a coral reef forms.

Hawksbill turtles live around Australia's Great Barrier Reef.

Enlarged picture of coral polyps with tentacles extended to catch tiny food particles.

Clown fish and sea anemone

Parrot fish eating staghorn coral.

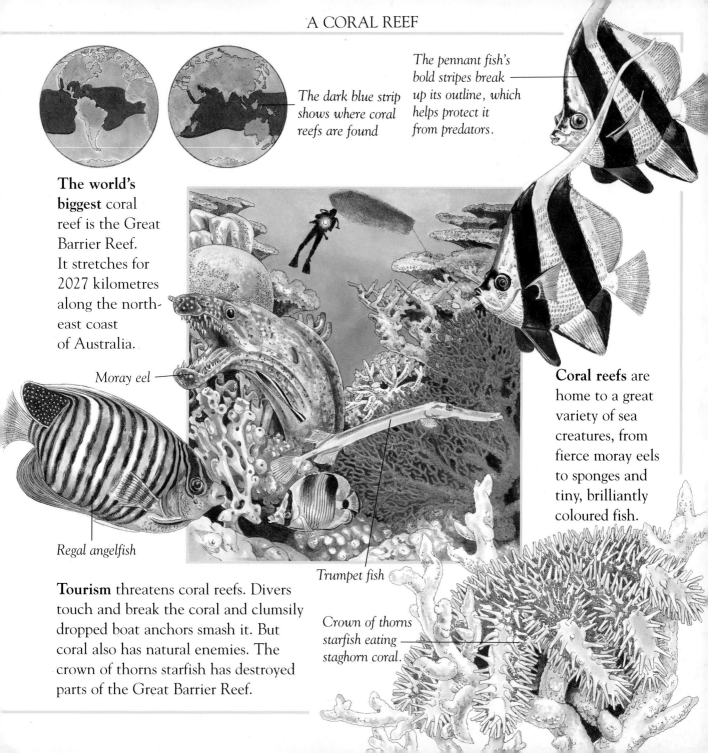

The dark blue strip shows where coral reefs are found

The pennant fish's bold stripes break up its outline, which helps protect it from predators.

The world's biggest coral reef is the Great Barrier Reef. It stretches for 2027 kilometres along the north-east coast of Australia.

Moray eel

Coral reefs are home to a great variety of sea creatures, from fierce moray eels to sponges and tiny, brilliantly coloured fish.

Regal angelfish

Trumpet fish

Tourism threatens coral reefs. Divers touch and break the coral and clumsily dropped boat anchors smash it. But coral also has natural enemies. The crown of thorns starfish has destroyed parts of the Great Barrier Reef.

Crown of thorns starfish eating staghorn coral.

Portuguese man-of-war

Close up of a drop of seawater

A bucket of seawater may look clear and empty, but it isn't. It will contain thousands of plants and animals too small to see without a microscope. These are the organisms that form plankton.

More species of plants and animals live close to the surface than anywhere else in the ocean. This is due to the Sun. All plants, whether they live on land or in the sea, need sunlight to make their food. So sea plants, which range from large seaweeds to microscopic diatoms, live at the surface where there is most sunlight. This means the sea animals that eat plants also live close to the surface most of the time.

Dolphin

*A black-headed gull
snatches a fish.*

*A shoal of mackerel
provides food for
many larger
creatures.*

*Violet
jellyfish*

Tuna

Ocean sunfish

Marlin

The ocean sunfish lives in
temperate and tropical seas. It is
almost completely round and grows to
4 metres. But even though it is big, it
can only feed on plankton, tiny fish and
jellyfish because its mouth is very small.

21

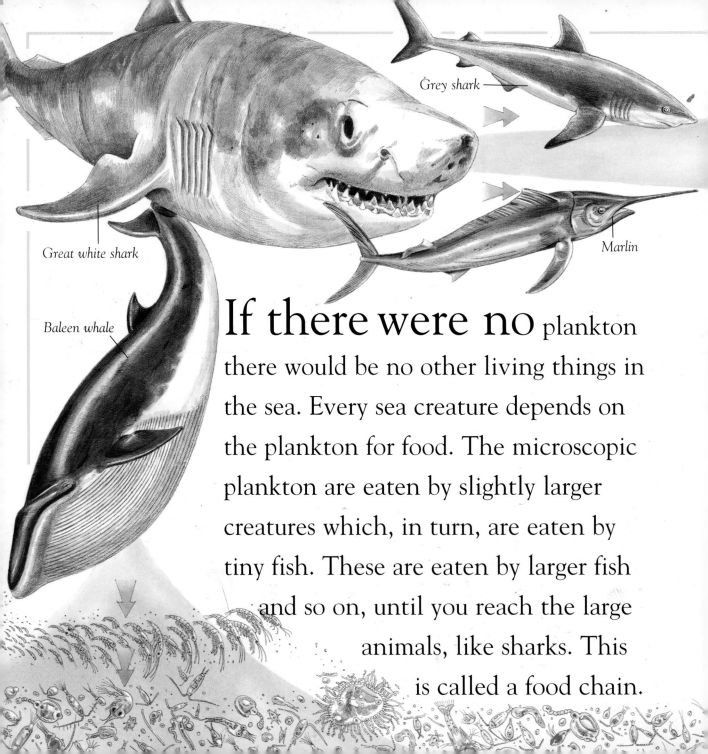

Grey shark

Marlin

Great white shark

Baleen whale

If there were no plankton there would be no other living things in the sea. Every sea creature depends on the plankton for food. The microscopic plankton are eaten by slightly larger creatures which, in turn, are eaten by tiny fish. These are eaten by larger fish and so on, until you reach the large animals, like sharks. This is called a food chain.

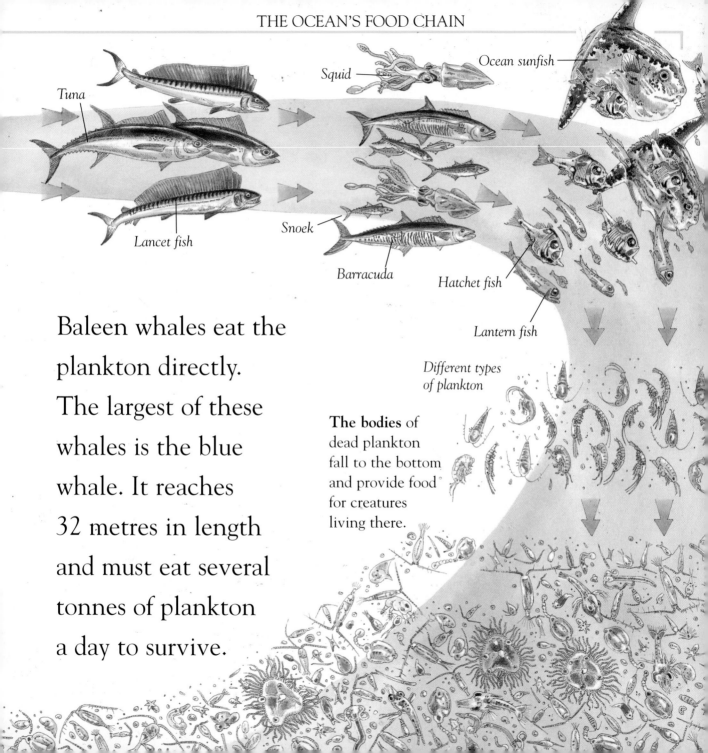

Tuna

Squid

Ocean sunfish

Lancet fish

Snoek

Barracuda

Hatchet fish

Lantern fish

Different types of plankton

The bodies of dead plankton fall to the bottom and provide food for creatures living there.

Baleen whales eat the plankton directly. The largest of these whales is the blue whale. It reaches 32 metres in length and must eat several tonnes of plankton a day to survive.

In 1690 Halley's diving bell descended 18 metres.

A diver in Lethbridge's armoured diving suit went down to 22 metres in 1715.

A diver reached 30.5 metres in 1872 wearing this suit.

First diving helmet, 1828

Exploring the deep

ocean is very difficult. There is no light, so explorers must take their own. It is also extremely cold so divers must be well protected. The pressure is so great that no human can survive and an ordinary submarine would be flattened. That is why the deep oceans are still almost unknown.

In 1943
Jacques Cousteau, a Frenchman, invented the aqualung. For the first time humans could breathe underwater.

Aqualung

In 1972 the *Alvin* (right), an American research submersible, descended 2 kilometres to explore the Pacific Ocean Ridge. It had a large camera mounted on an arm on the front, which extended to 60 metres.

Rat tail fish

Camera

Oarfish

Most deep-sea creatures move quite slowly, which makes photographing them easier.

Hatchet fish

Because the ocean is very dark, light cannot penetrate far. So cameras can only take close-up photographs of small creatures or small areas of the oceanbed.

Underwater camera

Viper fish

25

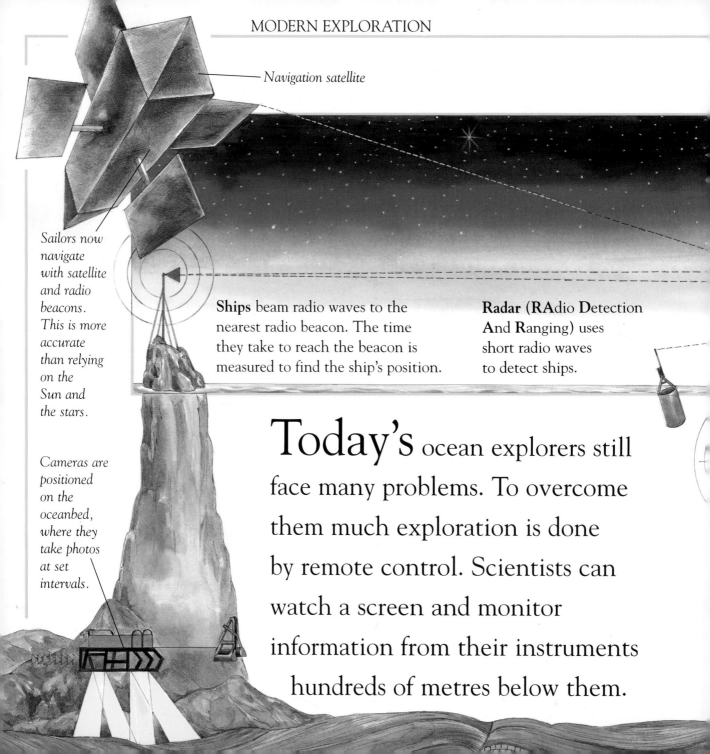

Navigation satellite

Sailors now navigate with satellite and radio beacons. This is more accurate than relying on the Sun and the stars.

Cameras are positioned on the oceanbed, where they take photos at set intervals.

Ships beam radio waves to the nearest radio beacon. The time they take to reach the beacon is measured to find the ship's position.

Radar (**RA**dio **D**etection **A**nd **R**anging) uses short radio waves to detect ships.

Today's ocean explorers still face many problems. To overcome them much exploration is done by remote control. Scientists can watch a screen and monitor information from their instruments hundreds of metres below them.

Sailors can navigate by looking at the stars

Oceanography is the study of the oceans. Oceanographic research vessels have all the equipment shown in the picture, but they would not use it all at once.

Instrument to measure echoes from undersea rocks

Oceanographic research vessel

Grab to collect oceanbed samples

A bathysonde measures water temperature and pressure, and how salty it is.

Sub-bottom echo sounding allows scientists to study rocks thousands of metres below the oceanbed. They use sounds and their echoes to build up a picture of the invisible rocks.

Dredges scrape material from the oceanbed for scientists to study what it is made of.

Corer taking oceanbed samples

Giant squid

The giant squid would be hard to imagine if you had not seen it. But describing it would be very difficult!

— *Coelacanth*

Coelacanths were thought to be extinct. Then, in 1938, a live one was caught off South Africa.

Male narwhals have a long spiral tusk, just like the horn of the mythical unicorn.

Even with modern technology exploring the oceans is difficult. So imagine what it must have been like for the first long-distance sailors in their tiny wooden boats, ocean-going canoes or rafts. Tired, hungry, dazzled by the Sun on a calm sea or peering through fog or the blackness of a storm, they 'saw' some very strange creatures. But not all were imaginary!

Narwhal

Manta ray

Dugongs live in shallow tropical seas. Because they often float upright in the water many people believe they were the original mermaids. But where is the long blond hair?

Dugong and young

Who would believe that a creature as odd as the hammerhead shark existed if they had not seen one? No wonder that people laughed at sailors' tales.

Hammerhead shark

Eye

29

Diver

Oyster bed

Section through oyster with a pearl

The sea and its creatures have always been used by people living close to it. Northern peoples have caught seals and whales for food, oil and furs for clothes. Tropical seas provided sponges and pearls. And there was fishing everywhere. These activities were on a fairly small scale, giving the coastal communities what they needed.

If a grain of sand gets into an oyster, the oyster makes a hard covering around the sand to stop it irritating. That is how pearls are formed. In Japan the pearl divers are always women, who dive without any special equipment – they just hold their breath!

Whalers

Traditionally the Inuit of Greenland and North America hunted seals with spears. Now they use rifles.

Harpoon

Hump back whale

Transporting dead seals is still done the traditional way — by sled.

When whales were hunted from small wooden boats, the hunters had to get close to their prey. Now they have big boats and high explosive rockets to fire harpoons from a safe distance. Many species of whales are now threatened with extinction.

It is not only the waters of the seas and oceans that have many resources. In many places the bed of the deep ocean is rich in manganese, a valuable mineral. Elsewhere, oil and natural gas lie below the oceanbed. Modern technology makes it possible to extract these natural resources, but it is extremely expensive and can be very dangerous. However, we need them because our modern way of life depends on these products. But oil and gas are 'fossil resources' – once they have been used up they do not form again.

When the rig is in position, all supplies are brought by ship.

Crane

Gulls look for food around rigs

Oil rigs are built at construction sites on the coast. Then they are towed to the site of the oil. They often stand a hundred metres above the sea. Most of the rig is underwater, anchored firmly to the oceanbed.

Revolving crane

Helicopter
landing pad

Gusts of wind
can smash
helicopters
against the rig.

Helicopters fly
the workers to
and from the rig.
In winter storms
this can be a
dangerous
operation.

Legs of rig

33

The smoke also causes pollution

Burning spilt oil

Oil is transported around the world in huge tankers. If one of these has an accident and spills the oil, the damage to the environment is enormous.

The world's seas and oceans are threatened, just as rainforests are on land. The increase in the world's human population means more demand for fish, oil and natural gas. It also means more waste from humans and their factories reaching the oceans and seas. All this threatens the balance of life that has evolved in them over millions of years.

Dying seal

Shore littered with oil and rubbish

Huge factory ships process the fish caught by fleets of trawlers.

Trawlers

Purse seine net

Many modern fishing nets have small mesh, so young fish cannot escape. This reduces the number of fish that will grow up and breed.

Oil suffocates fish. It clogs seabirds' feathers and seals' fur, so they are no longer waterproof – which means they will die.

Oil-clogged seabird

Creatures like dolphins are also caught in the huge nets. They, too, will die, although they are not used for food.

Dead fish

After the Sun, the sea is the most powerful constant influence on Earth. For years scientists have tried to find ways to use the energy in its waves and tides, but with very little success.

Out in the vast space of the deep mid-ocean tsunamis are often little bigger than normal waves.

Tidal waves or tsunamis are caused by undersea earthquakes and volcanic eruptions, often many kilometres from land.

The full destructive energy is only released when it sweeps up to land. Shallow coastal waters can force a tsunami up to a height of 65 metres.

Most tsunamis occur in the Pacific Ocean, because that is where most undersea eruptions and earthquakes take place. Tsunamis have reached speeds of 800 kilometres an hour – ordinary storm waves travel at about 55 kilometres an hour. A tsunami can cause enormous damage and many deaths if a region is densely populated.

USEFUL WORDS

Baleen Sheets of gristly material fringed with bristles which plankton-eating whales use to strain their food from the seawater.

Diatoms Microscopic plants found in plankton.

Equator An imaginary line around the centre of the Earth.

Hemisphere Half a sphere. The half of the Earth north of the Equator is the northern hemisphere and the half to the south is the southern hemisphere.

Mineral Any natural substance that has a set chemical make up. Gold and salt are minerals, but ordinary earth is not because its chemical make up varies.

Plankton Microscopic plants and animals that live in the seas and oceans.

Polar Cold region on land or sea near the North or South Poles.

Predator A creature that hunts for prey.

Prey A creature hunted for food.

Species Group of plants or animals that look alike, live in the same way and produce young that do the same.

Submersible A vessel that can travel at great depths underwater.

Temperate Climate that is not very hot, very dry, very cold or very wet. Found between tropical and polar regions.

Tropical Warm climatic region between latitudes 23° north and south of the Equator.

INDEX